Haven for Horses

by Tiffany Gibson

PEARSON

Glenview, Illinois • Boston, Massachusetts
Chandler, Arizona • Upper Saddle River, New Jersey

An **abandoned** horse stands alone in a field. He does not have a home. A horse that was *mistreated*, or treated badly, needs love. A horse that is hurt or sick needs medicine, but there is no one to help her. All of these horses need help. If no one helps them, they will die. Who will help these horses?

Horse havens help horses like these. Havens are safe places for animals. Horse havens **rescue** mistreated, abandoned, and sick horses. They give these horses love, food, medicine, and a home.

---

abandoned: left all alone without any care

rescue: save from harm or danger

Whinney Hill Farm

Whinney Hill Farm is a 20-acre farm in the country of Canada. This farm is special because rescued horses live there. Barbara Claussen owns Whinney Hill Farm. She rescues sick, hurt, or unwanted horses. She feeds the horses, gives them medicine, and finds new homes for them.

Barbara saved a horse named Dan. Dan had two broken legs, and his owner did not want him. Barbara bought Dan from his owner, and brought Dan to Whinney Hill Farm. Dan's legs healed with her care. Dan lived a happy life at Whinney Hill Farm for many years.

Dan and Barbara

veterinarian

Barbara Claussen rescued 62 horses from one farm. The farm owners used the horses to make medicine for people. When the farm closed, the owners did not want the horses. Barbara rescued all of the horses. She took them to Whinney Hill Farm.

The rescued horses were sick. A <mark>veterinarian</mark> said some of the horses might die. Barbara gave the horses medicine. She took care of them. All of the horses lived, and Barbara found new homes for them.

---

veterinarian: doctor for animals

Duchess Sanctuary

In California, Scott Beckstead also rescues horses. He is the *director*, or leader, of Duchess *Sanctuary*. A sanctuary is like a haven. It is a piece of land that is a safe place for animals. Duchess Sanctuary is a safe place for sick or unwanted horses.

Many groups bring horses to Duchess Sanctuary. One group is the Humane Society. The Humane Society rescues all kinds of animals. They bring rescued horses to Duchess Sanctuary.

Sometimes horse owners bring horses they do not want to the sanctuary. The owners do not have enough money to take care of the horses. The sanctuary workers give the horses food, water, and medicine. They give them a good home.

Havens rescue sick horses like this one.

Brighter Days Horse Refuge

Brighter Days Horse *Refuge* is a safe place for horses in Texas. A refuge is like a sanctuary or a haven. Jeannie and Bill Weatherholtz own this refuge. Like Whinney Hill Farm and Duchess Sanctuary, this place rescues horses. Jeannie and Bill give medicine to the sick horses and feed the hungry horses. Jeannie and Bill look for new homes for abandoned horses. More than 64 horses live at Brighter Days Horse Refuge.

Hungry horses eat well at horse havens.

Lucky

Havens help horses become healthy and happy.

Lucky 2 months later

Lucky is one horse at Brighter Days Horse Refuge. Someone brought him to a veterinarian. Lucky was very sick from eating a poison weed. The poison burned his skin. The veterinarian called Jeannie and Bill, and they agreed to take Lucky. The refuge gave him medicine, food, and a good home. Lucky is happy and healthy now.

A horse named Missy's Smile also has a home at Brighter Days Horse Refuge. When a group found Missy's Smile, she was hungry and sick. They brought her to the refuge. After two weeks at the refuge, Missy's Smile gained weight. Now she is happy and healthy too.

---

poison: something that can kill people and animals if it is swallowed

horseshoe

Helping Horse Havens

The Brighter Days Horse Refuge and other horse havens need money. They have to pay for food, medicine, and other supplies. Some havens pay veterinarians more than $400 every month to help the horses. They pay blacksmiths to make shoes for horses. Horses eat hay and grain. Some havens pay $1,450 a month for hay and grain.

How can horse havens get money and other help? Horse havens get the help they need in many ways.

Did You Know? Horses' Food

A 1,000-pound horse can eat more than 20 pounds of hay each day. But horses eat more than just hay. They also eat grass and other plants. They eat grains, such as barley and oats. Their owners add vitamins to their food too.

Donations

People donate money, time, and supplies to horse havens. These places have lists of supplies they need. People and businesses donate hay, medicine, blankets, and other supplies. A man named Brian Heinz donated more than two tons of hay to Duchess Sanctuary.

Many people give their time at horse havens. They go to the havens and help take care of the horses. They feed or ride the horses. A man named Jim Thorpe used his truck and trailer to bring sick horses to Duchess Sanctuary.

Some people give money to the horse havens. Most havens have Web sites. People give money through the Web sites. They also send money in the mail to horse havens.

hay

---

donate: give something as a gift

trailer

Sponsors sometimes get pictures of their horses.

Sponsors

Brighter Days Horse Refuge and other havens also use *sponsors*. A sponsor picks a horse. Then the sponsor gives money each month to help that horse. The refuge buys food, blankets, and other supplies for the horse. Some havens send pictures of the horses to their sponsors. They also send letters to tell the sponsors about the horses. Sponsors can visit their horses too.

Selling Items to Make Money

Brighter Days Horse Refuge also runs a shop. People donate furniture, dishes, and clothes to the shop. The shop then sells these things. Brighter Days Horse Refuge uses the money to take care of the horses.

Adopting a Horse

Many horse havens allow people to <mark>adopt</mark> horses. The havens find new homes for horses. People who want to adopt a horse go to a haven to meet a horse. They must have a large place where the horse can live. They must have enough money to feed and care for the horse. The new owners sign a paper. They promise to give the horse a good home. They promise to feed and take care of their new horse.

_____

adopt: take a person or animal into your family

People who adopt horses welcome them into their family.

You can help take care of horses at a haven.

How Can You Help?

Horse havens are important places. They rescue many horses every year, but the havens need people's help. Look for a horse haven in your area. Go to the haven and offer to help feed and care for the horses. Ask people to give money to a haven. Tell your friends and family about horse havens. With your help, horse havens can rescue many more sick, abandoned, and mistreated horses.